READ ALL ABOUT IT!

RACISM

ADAM HIBBERT

FRANKLIN WATTS
LONDON • SYDNEY

First published in 2001 by Franklin Watts
96 Leonard Street, London EC2A 4XD

Franklin Watts Australia
56 O'Riordan Street,
Alexandria, NSW 2015

Series editor: Rachel Cooke
Assistant editor: Adrian Cole
Designer: John Christopher, White Design
Picture researcher: Sue Mennell

A CIP catalogue record for this book is available from
the British Library.

ISBN 0 7496 4023 5

Dewey Classification 305.8

Printed in Malaysia

Acknowledgements:
Cartoons Andy Hammond pp. 22, 27; Sholto Walker pp. 14-15.
Photographs Front cover: PYMCA (Simon Norfolk) l; Popperfoto (Reuters/Simon Kreitem) tr; Rex Features (Paul Rogers) cra; Impact Photos (John Cole) crb; Popperfoto (Reuters/Grigory Dukor) br; Back cover: PYMCA (Simon Norfolk); Inside: Associated Press p. 11r; Bruce Coleman Collection p. 27 (Andy Price); Camera Press p. 21 (Richard Stonehouse); Commission for Racial Equality p. 22; Eye Ubiquitous p. 20b (Sportshoot); Format Photographers pp. 3tr (Joanne O'Brien), 6 (Brenda Prince), 19 (Joanne O'Brien), 26 (Lisa Woollet); ©The Guardian pp. 9 (Martin Argyles), 18 (Graham Turner), 20t (David Sillitoe); Impact Photos p. 16t (John Cole); Patrick Oliver pp. 3tl, 7; Peter Lomas p. 17; Peter Newark's American Pictures p. 12; Photofusion p. 24 (Bob Watkins); Popperfoto pp. 4 (Reuters/Simon Kreitem), 13, 16b (Anthony P. Bolante), 23 (Reuters/Kieran Doherty), 28 (Reuters/Jerry Lampen), 29t (Reuters/Grigory Dukor), 29b (Ady Kerry); PYMCA pp. 8 (Simon Norfolk); Rex Features pp. 3tc (Sipa), 3b (Photo News Service), 5 (Paul Rogers), 10 (Sipa/Juhan Kuus), 11l (Sipa); Ronald Grant p. 25

EDITOR'S NOTE

Read All About It: Racism takes the form of a newspaper called *The Racism News*. In it you can find a lot of articles about different subjects and many facts. It also includes opinions about these facts, sometimes obviously, as in the editorial pages, but sometimes more subtly in a news article: for example in the article concerning asylum seekers (page 7). Like any newspaper, you must ask yourself when you read the book 'What does the writer think?' and 'What does the writer want me to think?', as well as 'What do I think?'.

However, there are several ways in which *The Racism News* is not and cannot be a newspaper. It deals with one issue rather than many and it has not been published on a particular day at a particular moment in history, with another version to be published tomorrow. While *The Racism News* aims to look at the major issues concerning racism, the events reported have not necessarily taken place in the past few days but rather over the past few years. They have been included because they raise questions that are relevant to the issue today and that will continue to be so in the future.

Another important difference is that *The Racism News* has been written by one person, not many, in collaboration with an editor. They have used different 'voices' and, in some instances, such as the letters and the opinion column, pseudonyms. However, the people and events reported and commented on are real.

There are plenty of other things in *The Racism News* that are different from a true newspaper. Try looking at the book alongside a real newspaper and think about, not only where we have got the approach right, but where we have got it wrong! In the meantime we hope you enjoy reading *The Racism News*.

THE RACISM NEWS

Home News 7

Bishop in battle for immigrants

International News 11

Miss France mixed message

Education and Youth 19

Policing racism in schools

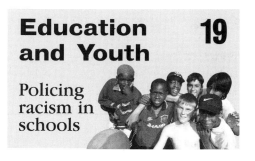

BRUTAL MURDER STILL CAUSING SHOCKWAVES

The News Editor

The murder of black teenager Stephen Lawrence in 1993 continues to throw racism into the headlines. The murder investigation, which failed to convict anyone, was severely criticised, and the Metropolitan Police accused of 'institutional racism' by the Macpherson Report.

The Police have had to review their attitudes and conduct, as have many other institutions. But now politicians are arguing over whether the Report has lead to a rise in violent street crime. Some claim incidents, such as the murder of 10-year-old Damilola Taylor in 2000,

Stephen Lawrence was stabbed to death in 1993.

are a result of the Police standing back to avoid further accusations of racism.

Solutions to the issues the Macpherson Report raised may not be easy. But it is sure to influence any debate on racism for years to come. ■

READ MORE: PAGES 4–6

Asylum Fears

Councils and refugee groups around the UK have revealed that asylum seekers are heading back to London and the south-east following their dispersal to cities like Glasgow and Newcastle. Nick Hardwick from the Refugee Council observes 'the system is in a critical condition'. The dispersal scheme, launched in April 2000, was designed to reduce the pressure experienced by many local authorities in southern regions. However, because of hostility in some areas, asylum seekers are returning south, according to Nick Hardwick: 'in fear of their lives.'

ASYLUM – FACTS AND DEBATES: PAGES 7–9

How It All Started

The facts you need to know about the murder of Stephen Lawrence and the events that followed

On 22 April 1993 a murderous attack that took place in South London left a family in tatters and a community in shock.

Black teenager Stephen Lawrence was brutally murdered while waiting for a bus with his friend, Duwayne Brooks. At around 10.30 p.m., a group of five or six white youths approached the two teenagers. Without any provocation they rushed at Stephen, who had walked away from the bus stop, in a swift and brutal racial attack.

During this incident Stephen was stabbed twice by one or more members of the group. The wounds, of about 17.5 centimetres in depth, severed main arteries in both his arm and chest. Massive bleeding resulted from these injuries. Despite this, Stephen managed to haul himself to his feet and run some 100 metres with Duwayne before eventually collapsing on the pavement. It was there, in Well Hall Road, that he died. The spot is now marked by a memorial stone.

RACIST MOTIVES

What started as a simple trip home eventually cost this young, talented boy his life. Charges were brought against two youths believed to be part of the murderous group that night. However, in July 1993, the Crown Prosecution Service (CPS) – the independent body that decides whether cases brought by the police should go to court – dropped the charges on the grounds of insufficient evidence.

In December 1993 the inquest into Stephen's death opened at Southwark Coroner's Court. It called five youths, all suspects in the case, to give evidence. But none of them did so, as they were not obliged to under law.

LACK OF EVIDENCE

The criminal prosecution had completely failed, and under current British law no one may be tried for the same crime more than once. In view of this, and the failure of the police to gather sufficient evidence, the Lawrence family decided to launch a private prosecution. Proceedings were opened at Greenwich Magistrate's Court in April 1994.

SICKENING ATTACK

Two years later the private prosecution concluded. New identification evidence in the case was ruled inadmissible. A verdict of unlawful killing was reached, but since evidence identifying suspects was not legally sound, it proved impossible to bring anyone to justice for Stephen's murder.

Although the suspects had not been named in the case the *Daily Mail* newspaper printed five names complete with photographs. It challenged the suspects to sue the newspaper if the allegations were false. A lawsuit has yet to be filed against the *Daily Mail*.

To determine exactly what happened and why so many mistakes were made a public inquiry, headed by Sir William Macpherson, was set up by the government in 1997. Five years after Stephen's murder it was hoped that the inquiry would address some of the unanswered questions, not least of which was 'Why are Stephen's killers still at large?'. It also looked at the police investigation, how it was conducted, and the subsequent failed prosecution of the suspects. ■

The Lawrence family sought justice in the courts.

NEW POLICE GUIDELINES

The departing Commissioner of the Metropolitan Police, Sir Paul Condon. He accepted claims of 'unintentional' racism in the Met.

The Metropolitan Police is being issued with a new guide to improve racism awareness as a result of the Stephen Lawrence Inquiry.

The new 129-page hand-book, *Guide to Identifying and Combating Hate Crime*, is being distributed among the Met's 25,000 employees.

A recent survey of police officers from ethnic minorities found that many felt themselves 'over-powered' by the culture of the force, which is 97% white. A recent United Nations report concluded that British police forces had a long way to go in improving their manage-ment of the race issue.

The guide is to be issued nationwide in England and Wales, following the issue of a similar booklet to Scottish police forces. ■

■ Professor Ellis Cashmore of Staffordshire University has completed a report which concludes that race recruitment targets set for the police in the wake of the Stephen Lawrence Inquiry should be scrapped.

SCRAP TARGETS

According to the report, black and Asian officers suspected that the targets were an easy option com-pared to other suggestions, such as taking police training and complaints procedures out of the hands of the police force. ■

Equality?

Over 30% of Londoners belong to an ethnic minority, but these minorities make up just 3% of the Metropolitan Police. ■

INVESTIGATING THE POLICE:

February 1997
■ Doreen Lawrence lodges formal complaint over the conduct of the Police Complaints Authority (PCA).

March 1997
■ PCA promises investigation.

July 1997
■ Home Secretary appoints Sir William Macpherson to chair a public inquiry.

December 1997
■ Scotland Yard's Superintendent Roderick Barker concludes that the police investigation had 'progressed satisfactorily and all lines of enquiry had been correctly pursued'.

March 1998
■ Macpherson begins public hearings and requests evidence from 5 white youths, identified as suspects during the case.

June 1998
■ Five white youths pelted with bottles and cans as they leave the public inquiry.

October 1998
■ Paul Condon, then Commissioner of the Met, apologises to the Lawrences, but denies that the police force suffers from 'institutional racism'.

February 1999
■ Macpherson Report published, and its seventy recommendations are welcomed by the Prime Minister and Home Office. Condon accepts the new definition of 'institutional racism' as 'unintentional'. Publication coincides with second PCA-sponsored internal inquiry by Kent Police. This concludes that the original investigation by the Metropolitan Police was 'seriously flawed'. ■

Police stop and search powers remain controversial among ethnic minorities.

Stop and search surprise

A Statewatch analysis of Home Office figures in the late 1990s found that 189 black people were stopped and searched per 1,000 black population, compared to the national average of 17 per 1,000 population as a whole. ■

Prison figures rise

Between 1985 and 1989, the non-white prison population of Britain rose from 5,723 to 7,229, representing an increase from 12% to 16% of the total prison population. ■

POLICE MUST BE FREE TO STOP AND SEARCH

Conservative leader, **William Hague has condemned guidelines** which make police reluctant to use their powers fully.

He said that the Stephen Lawrence Report had damaged the ability of police to maintain law and order, resulting in a rise in street crime.

The controversy has arisen over a particular policing method, known as 'stop and search'. This allows the police to stop people or cars and search them if they suspect a crime has been committed.

RISING CRIME

Stop and search has been criticised by anti-racist campaigners, because ethnic minorities tend to be targeted. One study found that non-whites are around eight times more likely to be stopped and searched than whites.

The Stephen Lawrence Report found 'clear, core evidence of racist stereotyping' in the use of stop and search powers.

This has lead to a drop in the use of the powers since the report, down 50% in London. In the same period, crime has risen.

Mr Hague believes that political correctness is making life less safe for the people it is meant to protect, and urges action. His call echoes a statement by his colleague Anne Widdecombe earlier in the year, when she said that the police must be allowed to 'do their job without automatically ending up in the wrong and in a disciplinary procedure'. ■

MAYORAL ADVISOR SLAMS ASYLUM POLICY

A key advisor to the Mayor of London has condemned the government's policies on immigration and asylum.

Lee Jasper, a former advisor to the Metropolitan Police on racism awareness, and secretary of the National Assembly Against Racism (NAAR), stresses the importance of asylum issues in the Assembly's annual report: 'The wave of hysteria about asylum seekers fuelled racism in every corner of society.

Racists everywhere crept out of the gutters and became more vocal and violent. A rise in racist violence was the direct consequence. Race crime figures for London in the year to April 2000 doubled.'

ASYLUM HYSTERIA

Mr Jasper noted that the problem was not confined to the capital city. Jan Passelbessi was murdered by racists in Newport, Gwent, and Glynne

Algard was murdered in Westbury, Wiltshire. The Welsh branch of the NAAR reported a 168% rise in racist incidents over the year.

The blame lay partly with the press, according to Mr Jasper. He referred to an Audit Commission report, *Another Country*, which found that in the months of October and November 1999, a sample of local press articles showed just 6% making 'any positive reference to asylum seekers or refugees'.

But in autumn 2000, the government eased its rules on immigration, partly as a response to a skills shortage in the UK. There was, said Mr Jasper, a 'calming of both the Tories' and the tabloids' rhetoric', which made it clear that the government 'had been setting this frightening agenda'.

Mr Jasper concluded that tough talk about cracking down on asylum seekers served to 'stigmatise and whip up racial hatred against asylum seekers and refugees. The government is creating the material conditions for racism.'

Mr Jasper dedicated the report to 58 illegal Chinese immigrants who suffocated to death in a container lorry in June 2000. ■

Bishop Joins the Battle

The Bishop of Croydon, the Rt Rev Wilfred Wood, has asked politicians to stop using language that echoes the provocative speeches of the late Enoch Powell in the 1960s and 70s.

CLIMATE OF FEAR

The Bishop, one of the most senior black members of the Church of England, regretted the anti-immigrant language used throughout 1999 and 2000. 'Black people's peace of mind does not figure very high

in our politicians' list of priorities,' he told the BBC Radio 4 Today programme.

The Bishop was adding his voice to those of a number of other prominent spokespeople, including the leader of the Transport Union, Bill Morris. Mr Morris recently called on the government to end its campaign against immigrants, which he said was creating a 'climate of fear' among ethnic minorities.

■ The Church Synod agreed to send the Archbishop of Canterbury and several other senior churchmen on a racism

Bishop Wood adds weight to chorus of disapproval.

awareness course at its 2000 meeting. Because of the lack of vicars from ethnic minorities some non-white Anglicans felt 'alienated and

lonely'. Between three and five times as many ethnic minority clergy were needed to reflect the changing make-up of church congregations. ■

ASYLUM ISSUE 'QUITE FUN' FOR RACISTS

A leading figure in the British National Party, Britain's main racist political group, has told supporters that the asylum issue makes their ideas more respectable.

Nick Griffin, the BNP leader, is quoted by the Anti-Nazi League as having told his supporters: 'The asylum seeker issue has been great for us. We have had phenomenal growth in membership. It has been quite fun to watch government ministers and the Tories play the race card in far cruder terms than we would ever use, but pretend not to. This issue legitimises us.'

Mr Griffin recently completed a two-year suspended sentence he received in May 1998 at Harrow Crown Court for incitement to racial hatred. He has described the Holocaust as a fiction created by '…Allied wartime propaganda, an extremely profitable lie, and latter-day witch hysteria.' ■

BNP supporters blame immigrants for many problems.

TORY STORM

M ichael Heseltine, thought to be one of the more liberal Conservatives, has caused a storm with his comments on asylum seekers in a recent interview for the BBC. While insisting he was not making racial remarks Mr. Heseltine, a former Tory deputy prime minister said: 'Let's not mince our language here. Why on earth should British citizens go without the houses they want, or take longer to get treatment they need, in order to make way for people who have cheated the immigration rules?'

INFLAMMATORY REMARKS

The remarks have been condemned by the Refugee League as 'inflammatory and prejudiced'. There has been a dramatic increase in the number of cases of racially-motivated violence. A Kosovan refugee who was attacked in Oxford said: 'At least when the Serbs attacked they were doing it because they wanted our homes. But here, we were just attacked for no reason.' ■

Asylum – the facts

■ In 1948 the British Nationality Act guaranteed 'Commonwealth Citizenship', including right of access to Britain, to all British subjects and Commonwealth countries – in all, about 950 million people. A series of limits was added to this Act throughout the 1960s and 70s, making almost all movement into Britain illegal except for those whose parents were born in the country, and for Irish citizens. The only exceptions are 'asylum seekers' – people fleeing persecution in their own countries whom Britain is obliged to look after under international human rights laws.

■ The Immigration and Asylum Act 2000 introduced the replacement of welfare benefits with a £35 per week food voucher system. It also saw the forced dispersion of asylum seekers around the UK and proposed to cut asylum decision waiting times to six months (from over 12 months).

■ Oxfam, Barnardo's, Shelter and Marie Curie have all withdrawn their support for the government's voucher scheme which leaves asylum seekers living below the poverty line.

■ Approximately half of Britain's non-white population was born and grew up in Britain.

■ Until officials stopped recording statistics in 1976, many more people left the UK than entered it every year. Between 1950 and 1975 only two years saw more immigrants than emigrants. Up to 80,000 more people a year were leaving than were moving to Britain.

■ Around 30,000 asylum applicants are allowed to stay in Britain each year.

■ Immigrant communities are typically 14% more economically productive than host communities. More than two thirds of independently-owned local shops are run by ethnic minority owners, and around 23% of Britain's doctors were born overseas. ■

Asylum applicants have undertaken rooftop demonstrations and hunger strikes in protest at their living conditions.

Dump the Camps

The News Editor

The Chief Inspector of Prisons has called detention centres for immigrants 'a complete and utter shambles'.

Sir David Ramsbotham drew particular attention to Campsfield House, a notorious high-security facility north of Oxford, which is privately run by security company Group 4.

UTTER SHAMBLES

According to Sir David's investigations, staff at Campsfield were unaware of their responsibilities and duties regarding care of the 'residents'. Though not officially prisoners or criminals, residents are required to remain within the camp's 20-foot perimeter fencing for as long as it takes for their asylum appeal to be heard – up to 18 months in some cases.

The Chief Inspector finds that the resulting confusion over inmates' rights causes conflict and results in the centres being 'unsafe for detainees'.

The pressure group Asylum Rights Campaign notes that troublemakers are moved to regular prisons, where their treatment is even worse.

STAFF 'UNAWARE'

Campsfield's local MP, Evan Harris, says: 'It is clear that this country detains far too many, for far too long, at far too young an age in many cases, without giving a good reason, without judicial oversight, under the wrong regimes and with inadequate safeguards.' ■

■ Labour and Conservative MPs have been referred to the Commission for Racial Equality over concerns about the language used in the asylum debate. ■

■ Leading Conservative MP Anne Widdecombe has been 'flanned' – struck by a flying pastry – at a book signing in Oxford. Protestors calling themselves the Campsfield High Command of the Biotic Baking Brigade aimed the sweet pastry at the MP to draw attention to alleged racism in local election leaflets issued by her party. The leaflets allegedly raised the prospect of 'asylum racketeers flooding the country with bogus asylum seekers'. Protestor Bill Turner, 20, claimed that: 'Both main political parties are using the race card to win support.' ■

Hell Hounds

International Editor

An international expert on dog training has called for 90% of South Africa's police dogs to be destroyed.

His call came as the world was shocked by video footage of immigrants in South Africa being viciously attacked by police dogs. Six white police officers were tried for attempted murder for their part in the barbaric attack.

Hans Schegel, who runs a world-famous police dog training school in Switzerland, told BBC journalists that the dogs were clearly 'trained on fear' and had 'no trust in human beings'.

The training methods used were at least 50 years behind those used by police forces in Europe, and had produced dogs which could never be retrained. The only option was to destroy them and start from scratch.

TRAINED ON FEAR

Mr Schegel noted that the training employed racist techniques, and new dogs should only be trained by 'emotionally stable' dog handlers.

The international trainer had consulted with the South African police in previous years, but was told that changes were not possible because of a lack of money. ■

RACISM REMAINS

Nelson Mandela, the former President of South Africa, has attacked his country's new black establishment for racism. Speaking in an interview with the Johannesburg *Sunday Times*, Mr Mandela warned: 'A sense of insecurity among Indians, mixed race and white minorities is being fuelled by careless black leaders.' In February 2001, just a week before Mandela's interview was published by the paper, the country's lottery boss Edmund Radebe was reported casting doubt on the Asian community's sense of responsibility. But as Mandela points out, his black majority party, the African National Congress, should be committed to supporting the interests of all South Africans, regardless of colour. 'However harsh apartheid was,' he goes on, 'these groups found a niche for themselves. With change, the insecurity that grips minority groups is worsening.'

The elder statesman of the new South Africa was careful not to point the blame at particular black leaders, but insisted: 'The ANC has to do something...South Africa belongs to all who live in it, black and white.'

■ Housing Department chief Carien Engelbrecht has announced a £125 million plan to rebuild one of the country's most overcrowded townships. Alexandra, northeast of Johannesburg, with an infra-structure to support 70,000 inhabitants, is presently occupied by around 350,000 people, 60% of whom are unemployed. The move is one of seven urban renewal projects prioritised by President Thabo Mbeki. ■

Confrontations with armed police are still commonplace.

RACISME, MADEMOISELLE?

Some French employers have missed the anti-racism message

The crowning of Mlle Sonia Rolland as the new Miss France was marked with controversy.

Mlle Rolland, 18, was representing the Burgundy region, but represented much more to the television station organising the contest.

TF1, France's leading TV channel, has been dogged by complaints about the lack of presenters from ethnic minorities. TF1's new Miss France has one Rwandan parent, and is 'half black'.

No sooner had she been crowned than Genevieve Fontenay, the (white) presenter of the show, happily declared to the viewers that 'France is not racist'.

Perhaps her audience was small – some French employers seem to have missed her message. A recent study by French anti-racist pressure group, SOS-Racisme, found that ethnic minorities were grossly discriminated against. French citizens of Arab descent were routinely treated as an underclass.

An SOS-Racisme volunteer contacted several employers pretending to look for work, using the first name Muhammad – suggesting Arab descent. The same volunteer also submitted identical job applications, but changed the first name to François – which hinted that he was white. 'François' was invited to interviews, 'Muhammad' was not.

DISCRIMINATION

In the meantime, a rival Miss France organisation has elected an alternative beauty. She's from Calais, and blonde. ■

Sonia Rolland brings the debate to a new audience.

POTATO ROASTED

A statue of a Mr Potatohead character has been removed from Rhode Island, USA, after complaints that it promoted racial prejudice.

The character, 'Tourist Tater', was one of several artworks commissioned by the island to promote tourism – Rhode Island is the home of the company that makes the toy 'Mr Potatohead', as seen in Disney's blockbuster films *Toy Story* and *Toy Story 2*.

Tourist Tater was heavily-tanned, wore bad-taste clothes and grinned madly (see picture, right); as such, some felt it was too close to caricatures such as 'Little Black Sambo' and the 'gollywog', long associated with racist attitudes.

Onna Moniz-John, the area's affirmative action officer, said that the only thing

missing to complete the racist image was a watermelon.

But the artist, Kathy Szarko, was amazed at the reaction. 'He's a potato. That's why he's brown,' she said.

Other sculptures left standing include 'Edgar Allen Poe-tato', a tribute to the 19th-century gothic poet and novelist who briefly lived in the area. ■

History is Never Black and White

Ideas of racial superiority have existed at least since the Middle Ages in Europe. In feudal kingdoms, run by a monarch and a small band of aristocrats, the peasantry who made up the labour force were thought to be an inferior race.

At the same time, Jewish communities in Europe were widely despised and hated by their Christian neighbours. Attacks and even massacres took place, justified on religious and racial grounds, although in reality there was often a financial motive behind them.

SLAVES TO THE AMERICAS

As European countries began to industrialise and to colonise the Americas in the 17th and 18th centuries, two important changes took place. On the one hand, Africans were taken captive and made into slaves to provide cheap labour in the plantations of the Americas. On the otherhand, ideas of democracy, equality and freedom for all began to emerge, finding expression in the American War of Indpendence and the French Revolution. Slavery was widely condemned, but some countries relied on it for their wealth. It took a civil war in America to free the last slaves.

PROBLEMS OF INEQUALITY

Racism did not disappear though. The Industrial Revolution had not solved problems of inequality, and race offered a convenient explanation for people's differing success. In the 1930s, Hitler's Nazi party exploited these beliefs to gain power in Germany. Their policies led to the Holocaust of World War II. After the

Europeans shipped Africans to America as slaves to work the plantations.

Allied victory, racism was condemned as dangerous and inhuman, and Western opinion turned strongly away from politics that supported it. The United Nations was established and an international standard of human rights was agreed by all the member countries.

Reflecting the post-war mood, Britain opened its borders to other Commonwealth citizens. But by the 1960s, immigration restrictions were introduced. Only those whose parents or grandparents had been born in Britain could immigrate. Immigrants began to find themselves blamed for shortages of jobs and houses and a new wave of racism swept through Britain.

Despite this racial tension, new influences were felt in Europe. Black American leaders, such as Martin Luther King, showed how non-whites were still treated unfairly in 'white' countries. They ensured that it became illegal to discriminate against someone because of their race, and saw to it that racist regimes around the world, such as that in South Africa, were widely condemned.

The importance of ethnic, as opposed to racial, difference became more recognised in the 1980s and 90s. Schools began to teach children about ethnic groups, and encouraged them to see things from other people's viewpoint. It hasn't ended racism but it has given a new perspective to its history and the debates that surround it. ■

TIMELINE

Through the ages different events have shaped the world we live in today.

1561
John Hawkins becomes first British slave trader to the Spanish West Indies.

1770s
Industrial Revolution builds up head of steam. More and more people move to towns and cities for work.

1770–1820
Ideas of freedom and equality for all grow in strength. These are expressed in the French Revolution of 1789.

1791
Slaves revolt on Haiti and seize the island from the French, leading France to abolish slavery in 1794.

1805
British control of India firmly established.

1807
William Wilberforce MP wins campaign to abolish slavery in the British Empire.

1820s
Intellectual trends in Europe turn towards ideas of nation and race.

1858
Indian 'mutiny' against British army.

1859
Darwin's *Origin of Species* published. His theory of 'survival of the fittest' adds fuel to the race debate.

1865
The American Civil War is won by the North, resulting in the abolition of slavery in the United States.

1866
Ku Klux Klan founded in America to intimidate freed slaves and crush civil rights activity in the South.

1880s, 90s
The 'scramble for Africa' – European powers colonise the continent.

1933–1945
Adolf Hitler and the Nazi Party rule in Germany. Their anti-semitic and racist policies lead to the Holocaust.

1947
India and Pakistan gain independence from British rule. Commonwealth citizenship granted to all British subjects.

1948–57
Approximately 300,000 Commonwealth citizens immigrate to Britain.

1962–71
Immigration controls tighten to apply to those with roots in Britain, i.e. white Commonwealth citizens only.

1964
Martin Luther King wins the Nobel Peace Prize for his role in winning civil rights for black Americans.

1967
World Champion boxer Muhammad Ali refuses the draft to fight in Vietnam.

1968
Martin Luther King assassinated. Racial intergration policies begin to be replaced with multicultural approach.

1976
Race Relations Act introduces an offence of 'incitement to racial hatred' in Britain.

1981–5
Riots in major British cities, provoking review of race relations by Lord Scarman.

1994
South Africa extends the vote to black citizens – Nelson Mandela elected president.

2000
Cathy Freeman, of Aboriginal descent, lights the Torch at the Sydney Olympic Games. ■

Martin Luther King battled for equal rights.

Editorial

STICKS AND STONES

The fuss about what the Runnymede Trust report says about Britain (page 20) is itself a sign of the problem. This country is obsessed with seeming tolerant and democratic, to the point that anyone who suggests otherwise is not tolerated and denied their democratic rights.

But when did racism become an issue of using the right vocabulary? When did it stop being about the fact – still relevant in this century – that ethnic minorities are treated as second-class citizens?

To the civil rights leaders of the 1960s such as Martin Luther King, the important thing was to prevent the state being used to keep minority races down. By demanding equality in the law, blacks were empowered to stamp out inequalities elsewhere. They demanded this power for their own purposes.

But there's a new anti-racism in town, now. This version says that racism creates victims, too weak to be left to fend for themselves. Instead of correcting the inequalities of our justice system, this version prefers to help victims with their mental scars.

Instead of preventing the police from harassing young blacks and Asians, it offers counselling and anger management training for the kids on the receiving end.

This is not anti-racism, just good old-fashioned thought-control.

It's time we stopped being impressed by kind words, and pressed instead for firm action! ■

Letters

Adoption Hope?

Dare we hope that the government's review of adoption in Britain will address the question of race? For too long now, willing parents and needy children have been kept apart by an adoption service which refuses 'inter-racial' adoption.

Hundreds of black children go unadopted because not enough black couples can be found to take them, while willing white parents are told that there are no 'suitable' children for them to care for.

Of course white parents can't teach their child about racism from their own experience. But they can show them love and provide firm family support in ways a care home never will. Which is more important for the child's interests?

Let's hope this government enforces some common sense.

[name and address withheld]

Plenty for Everyone

For a so-called Christian country, it seems odd to me that many Britons believe that immigrants are bad people who should be turned away.

The common sense arguments are anything but. My favourite is the one about Britain being too over-crowded. If you really believed that, you'd spend more on birth control and getting people to retire to Spain or somewhere.

My faith says 'For every mouth to feed, God gave a pair of hands' – so why see strangers as a burden when they also offer opportunity?
Fraternally,
Morris Merrier

EARN TO 'MANAGE' YOUR ANGER...

DICTIONARY OF PLATITUDES

Shotto Walker

Political Correctness Gone Mad

How typical of your politically correct paper to spout such nonsense about immigration controls being racist.

The plain fact of the matter is that Britain is a small island, already overburdened by the existing population.

Opening the doors to everyone can only lead to urban chaos and environmental disaster. There is no racial element to this observation. It's just mathematics.

Sincerely,

P. C. Knott

No More Roving?

If immigration controls are colourblind, why have the Irish always been allowed free entry to Britain?

Yours,

Mary Monaghan

IN MY OPINION

"Has Multiculturalism Failed?"

Multiculturalism. *Noun*. The theory of race relations which promotes equality by respecting and supporting the separate cultural identity of different ethnic groups.

We read so much information on the issues surrounding racism. It seems to suggest that we can take action against racism simply by celebrating and emphasising the ethnic differences between different people. Society is, after all, made up of numerous cultures and communities from different corners of the world. Initially it seems a good idea to identify these groups so that we can begin to understand the differences. But this form of multiculturalism only supports, and even helps, to spread racist ideas.

By teaching people to look at an individual's ethnic background rather than his or her own achievements, character and values, race becomes the first thing people look at, sometimes even before identifying them as male or female!

RACIAL IDENTITY

Many so-called 'affirmative action' schemes, developed from multicultural initiatives, have been dropped precisely for this reason. In California, USA, colleges and universities that stopped giving preferential treatment to ethnic minority recruitment actually saw an improvement in year-on-year figures. Individual students felt more confident studying at these institutions because they were there on their own merits, achievements and success, not because of a government policy. In other words, multiculturalism can serve to hold ethnic minorities back from their individual potential.

LOW CONFIDENCE

Individuals become trapped by the labels given to them, for example 'black', 'Hispanic', etc. Multiculturalism builds barriers between different people by separating them into different ethnic groups. Divisions which are made only by race, which when used in everyday 'politically correct' conversation, weaken the power of the individual. Parties such as the British National Party can seize on these definitions. One posting on its website explained: 'We do not hate foreigners. We simply want to preserve the unique flavour of English communities and the traditions of local culture.' Some politicians have also explained their attitude to immigration in similar terms, worried that the influence of too many other cultures will some how corrupt the British way of life.

COLOURBLINDNESS

It is hardly surprising that racially-motivated violence and other incidents are on the increase again. Largely because of 'political correctness' we cannot be colourblind to individual's ethnic background. It is at the front of our mind every time we communicate with someone.

We must move away from ideas of ethnic diversity and collective identity towards celebrating the individual and his or her own merits. In order to eradicate racism, we must change the way we look at the world from within our own minds.

Yours,

Prof. A. Sceptic

BRITAIN LAGS BEHIND U.S.

Where are Britain's African–Caribbean businessmen and women?

Are boxing (Lennox Lewis) and modelling (Naomi Campbell) still the best chance of success for young black Britons?

Annual indexes of wealthy people are seldom a good guide to social trends. But the latest *Times* 1000 list reflects an interesting disparity

between white, Asian and black success. It seems that African-Caribbean talent is still going unrewarded. Asian entrepreneurialism seems to be alive and well on the other hand. Rich lists detail multimillionaire Asians as young as 26 year-old Ajaz Ahmed, already commanding a £12 million fortune. Is there a case for discrimination here?

UNREWARDED

Black business in America is becoming a major success story. Pioneering entrepreneurs in the entertainment industry – the moviemaker Spike Lee and the founder of Def Jam

Records, Russell Simmons, for example – are being followed by growing numbers of African-American executives and business-owners.

Take Anthony Parks, of Oakland, California. Having worked hard and got in 'at the bottom' of an Internet business that did well, the 40-something black businessman has earned enough in share options to begin sharing the joy. So far he has given about one million dollars' worth of shares to old friends.

But in Britain, meanwhile, *The Times* Rich List's only wealthy black businessman has been Carl Cushnie – now battling to stay clear of a financial scandal engulfing the company that made him his money. ■

*Why are black business men/ women
so thin on the ground in the UK?*

COKE – THE REAL THING

The Coca Cola corporation has settled a race dispute with representatives of its workforce worth almost $200 million.

The company has agreed to pay $192.5m to correct a poor record on pay rates and promotions for black employees, after four workers took it to a tribunal.

Doug Daft, Coca Cola Chairman, said 'Today we have closed a painful

chapter in our company's history.'

The money is to be divided between cash compensation to recent employees, adjusting salaries for existing employees and investing in new procedures for recruitment and personnel management.

■ Seven African-Americans have launched a similar suit against Microsoft, the computing corporation. An initial price tag of $5 billion

***Bill Gates's company
Microsoft faces lawsuit.***

has been set for their claims. Microsoft is expected to reject the case outright. ■

WHITES WIN RACE CASE

■ Two white council employees have won thousands of pounds compensation from a tribunal which ruled that they suffered racial discrimination from black colleagues.

Ian Short and James Monaghan accepted an offer from Lambeth Council to settle the case after the court was told how they were forced from their jobs in 1996 after a campaign of racial discrimination.

Their manager, a black woman, treated them as inferior to their eight colleagues, all of whom were black women. Mr Monaghan was used as a 'white face' and a 'white voice' for the Council in the department's dealings with the public.

A spokesperson for the Commission for Racial Equality confirmed that a small handful of approximately 1,700 cases each year involve claims by whites against ethnic minority managers or employers. ■

EQUAL OPPS JUS'T WHITEWASH?

Researchers at Cardiff University Business School have found shocking evidence that big companies with equal opportunities policies are more likely to discriminate against ethnic minority employees.

Kim Hoque and Dr Mike Noon conducted the survey by sending speculative job applications to each of the top 100 companies listed in the *Times* 1000 directory of companies.

NO OBLIGATION

Each of the companies received two application forms: one from 'Andrew Evans', and one from 'Ramesh Patel'.

In general, the 'Ramesh Patel' application received a less informative or positive response.

The authors of the report, *Racial Discrimination in Speculative Application*, also made a surprise discovery. Of the companies that emphasised their fairness to ethnic minorities, 42% of responses to 'Mr Patel' were inferior to the responses the 'white' candidate received.

But companies which made no statement about their equal opportunities policy actually discriminated less often – just 22% of their responses to 'Mr Patel' were inferior.

Dr Noon concludes that companies may be claiming to be fair because it is good for their image. There is no legal obligation for them to prove their claims, or even to keep track of the problem. ■

How one family's dream turned into a nightmare in just 24 hours

Mal & Linda – Standing Tall

Business Editor

Mal Hussain and his partner Linda sold everything to buy their business – Ryelands Mini Market on the Ryelands Estate, Lancaster.

They opened for business in June 1991. On the first day, Mal was called a 'black monkey', within a week he had been threatened with a knife, and by November 1991 mobs of up to 100 people were gathering outside the shop after dark and pelting windows with stones and bricks.

In at least one instance, police responded to the couple's 999 call the following morning.

Customers were also threatened and warned not to use the shop. On November 10th 1996, long after the couple had turned their home into a fortress of steel shutters and razor wire, a number of customers, including an asthmatic, were trapped inside the shop when a burning mattress was wedged against the door.

3,000 ATTACKS

Since 1994, the couple have kept a diary of incidents in an attempt to persuade authorities to act. The diary details over 3,000 separate attacks, from the stoning of customers to an attempted stabbing of Mal and several arson attacks.

The City Council's response to the problem was to advise the couple to move. Compensation for the loss of their business – their

Linda and Mal's business survives against all odds.

entire life savings – was so small that the couple could not afford to accept it, even if they had chosen to.

Just one resident has been asked to leave a council property on the Estate as a result of the decade of racial abuse by hundreds of locals.

But through it all, Mal and Linda have managed to hold on to one plain fact: 'We just believe that we have done nothing wrong.' In demanding nothing more than the right to live their lives in peace, they are an example to us all. ■

ANTI-RACISM FOR WHITES

When Leah Levane confronted a group of 40 or 50 angry young white men outside the Bede House Adventure Project in Bermondsey in 1992, she made a small breakthrough.

The youth centre had narrowly survived an arson attack. The young men were full of anger, but after talking for just a few minutes, Leah discovered that their racism was only skin deep. Confronting their prejudices was easier than she had expected.

'Gradually, as we talked, you could see one or two start to think about what they were saying.'

FULL OF ANGER

The experience set her thinking. According to the British Crime Survey, 25% of racist attacks, 60% of racially-motivated vandalism and 30% of all cases of racial abuse are carried out by white teenagers. Yet very few anti-racist projects work with disadvantaged white boys.

With a grant from the National Youth Agency, Ms Levane recruited former National Front member Ray Barker to help in an outreach project.

'I knew all the BNP lines from my days,' Ray recalls. 'The leaders lived outside London, and would come in, create the trouble and then leave us to deal with the police.' Ray knew all about the frustrations of poverty in inner cities, and the easy answers racist politics seemed to offer.

'We believed that racism wasn't all there was about them,' says Ms Levane. 'These young people were also incredibly deprived, and had all sorts of problems of their own.' Racist incidents on the estates covered by the scheme dropped by 46% over three years, while incidents elsewhere were on the increase.

ONLY SKIN DEEP

The project had to end, and the lesson has yet to be applied across the country with any regularity. 'What we did was a drop in the ocean,' Levane says. 'But it was important to do something.' ∎

A new marking system should stamp out even subconscious racism by examiners.

BLIND JUSTICE

A pilot scheme for the marking of anonymous A Level papers aims to stamp out racism in examiners' judgements in the vital exams.

The Qualifications and Curriculum Authority said it was taking the findings of the Stephen Lawrence Inquiry seriously by making it impossible for examiners to guess candidates' ethnic backgrounds from details included with the completed papers, including both their names and the details of the colleges they were studying at.

Dennis Oppos, the Authority's senior manager, said, 'It's a system that's been in place for a number of years now in Northern Ireland, and we're hoping that it will be introduced in the near future in England.' ∎

Macpherson Report: Could Do Better

The headmaster of a Bedford school has spoken out against the dangers of the Macpherson Report.

Mike Berrill, head of Biddenham Upper School, in the Bedford Education Action Zone, warns that the Macpherson Report's proposals and definitions will lead to meaningless anti-racism measures.

Schools across the country are adopting racist incident forms in an attempt to fulfil their responsibilities as public bodies to prevent institutional racism, which the Report defines as any arrangement that results in one ethnic group being disadvantaged in any way.

UNEQUAL OUTCOME

As Mr Berrill told the *Times Education Supplement*, 'An inspection report described my school's multi-ethnic harmony as an outstanding strength. We expend great energy trying to understand and counteract racism. But despite this, the unequal outcomes of my students, whether Indian, Pakistani or Bangladeshi, etc. we are, by definition, institutionally racist.'

A similar nonsense arises out of Macpherson's definition of a racist incident as being any event that any witness perceives to have been racist.

School pupils of all ethnic backgrounds, not least white Britons, are very capable of exploiting this opportunity to cause mischief for staff by accusing them of racism. Mr Berrill suggests that, with terms this loose and meaningless, the serious charge of racism could lose its meaning. ■

Will the Report interfere with these kids' education?

High rate of school exclusion

Approximately 7.1% of all permanent exclusions from schools in 1995/6 were of African-Caribbean pupils, though they constitute only 1.5% of the total school population. ■

MEDIA REACTION TO RACE REPORT 'WAS RACIST'

Professor Parekh became the target of media outrage.

An author of a major survey of racism in Britain has condemned the newspaper reporting of his findings.

Professor Bikhu Parekh spoke out at a conference of the National Union of Journalists in defence of the report, *The Future of Multi-Ethnic Britain*, commissioned by the Runnymede Trust.

The 416-page report made headlines when two newspapers, the *Daily Telegraph* and the *Daily Mail*, claimed that the report branded all white Britons racist.

'We said that the term British had attracted racial connotations,' Professor Parekh said. 'They misread it as "racist" with, I think, a certain amount of prejudice.

'We just meant that the word is associated with white people, which has been said hundreds of times before. But the stories led to a grave injustice.' He had received around 120 offensive and threatening letters, and staff at the Runnymede Trust had received abusive phone calls.

The Trust is no stranger to run-ins with the press. In 1989 its report, *Daily Racism*, demonstrated links between tabloid scare stories on Asian immigrants and racially-motivated murders. ∎

Survey Reveals Dangerous Myths

Britons are shown to be dangerously mis-informed about ethnic minorities.

A survey of attitudes conducted by *Reader's Digest*, a non-political monthly magazine, has shed light on the roots of racism in modern Britain.

The readership of upwardly-mobile working class and middle class consumers responded to questions on a wide range of issues. Questions about race and immigration were particularly revealing:

∎ Two out of three people replying to the survey said that Britain was too generous to new arrivals in the UK. But their attitudes appeared to be based on false information.

∎ Respondents guessed that roughly 26% of the British population were recent immigrants, as opposed to the true figure of 7%. Respondents believed press stories that asylum seekers were receiving up to £113 per week each from the government, when in fact the voucher system allocates each adult £36.54, of which a mere £10 may be converted to cash.

∎ Eighty per cent of readers believed that Britain is 'a soft touch' for asylum seekers. Yet just 10,000 out of more than 70,000 applications were approved in 1999, and applications to other European countries ran significantly higher than those to Britain. ∎

Journalists need networks

A prominent black journalist has demanded that newspaper editors and the public stop treating journalists from ethnic minorities as 'race experts'.

Gary Younge, a *Guardian* journalist, says he is tired of people making the assumption that race must be the only issue he is interested in.

'If you are black and you do stories about race then you are a "race journalist", but race is not a side issue. There are black people involved in all issues,' he said.

His comments were reinforced by Busola Odulate, a reporter for *The Sunday People*. 'There's always been pressure on me to go for campaigning journalism and for a while I tried it but it was not what I wanted to do ... more young black journalists should be encouraged to go into the tabloids. We're not all broadsheet journalists.'

Mr Younge believes the 'institutional' problem of racism in newspapers is partly a result of the way journalists are recruited.

Editors 'hire people in their own image, and there are no black editors. They hire people they hear about at dinner parties. We are not asking for access to dinner parties, but for recruitment to be done in an open way,' he said. 'But as long as the system works the way it does young people are going to have to go along with it and we're going to have to help them. We're going to have to start networking like the Lawsons do' – referring to a successful family of white media personalities. ■

RACIST MEDIA AGENDA

An article that appeared recently in the Australian newspaper the *Sydney Morning Herald* has been highlighted as an example of the type of reporting that needs to be stamped out in the 21st century.

LACKING IN FACTS

The piece, titled 'Korean Inc.', focused on alleged Asian gang-related violence in Sydney and the increase in the number of brothels in what was called a crime war. According to the Green-Left Party, the article was lacking in facts and supporting evidence, and was clearly produced simply to spur on newspaper sales on a slow news day. A Party spokesperson said: 'Headlines such as "Korean gangs blamed for new city crime wave" simply stir-up aggressive nationalist sentiments. It makes unmistakably clear that even the so-called "quality" papers quite consciously pursue a racist agenda.'

ASIANS BLAMED

Perhaps the next time an Australian is arrested at Bangkok airport for drugs smuggling the headline should read 'Drug Runners: Australian Inc.'? ■

Networking like the Lawsons – parties are a great way to make new contacts.

CELEBRITY – ONLY SKIN DEEP?

Famous British faces have undergone computer-enhancement to make them appear to be a different race, in a new awareness campaign from the Commission for Racial Equality.

Spice Girl Mel B, ginger DJ Chris Evans and nightclub impresario Peter Stringfellow are among the celebrities who speak through their new skin to challenge viewers about their racial prejudices.

Sports personalities Naseem Hamed and Lennox Lewis don a pale complexion – Hamed even takes blue eyes – in the adverts, while Chris Evans appears as a slightly odd-looking African-Caribbean.

According to Kai Hsiung, one of the boffins behind the special-effects short films, Chris Evans was especially pleased with his new image. He asked if he could keep his make-up on to play a joke on a friend in hospital.

Mel B said, 'Hopefully this as will have an impact and sink in because it's so dramatic. Britain is very multicultural and we're stupid to think we can ignore it.' ■

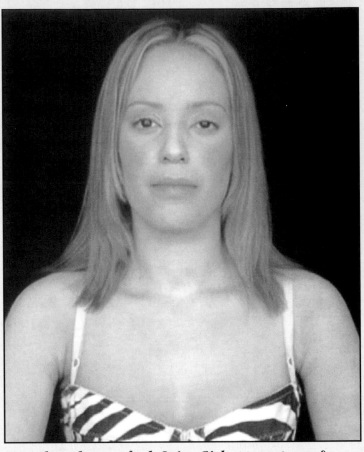

How does the new-look Spice Girl appear to you?

The Black Prince

INCREDIBLE, I NEVER THOUGHT THEY WOULD LET A WOMAN PLAY JULIET!

The Theatre Critic

The Royal Shakespeare Company (RSC) has made history by having an English king played by a black actor.

David Oyelowo has been hailed as 'the black Olivier' – after the RSC's adored leading man, Laurence Olivier – and stars as Henry VI in a new RSC production of the three-part play, *Henry VI*.

As Oyelowo puts it: 'You don't question a white actress playing Cleopatra, even though she is supposed to be an Egyptian. If I'm on stage and say I'm in tears, you believe me. If I say I've got an army of 30,000 offstage, you believe me. I don't know why if I say I'm the King of England that is suddenly so much more controversial.'

Shakespeare's plays have often caused controversy in casting – choosing which actors to use. The most famous role for black actors is Othello, the tragic, noble warrior betrayed by one of his advisors into murdering the woman he loves. For centuries the part had been played by white actors wearing black make-up. It's now just as rare to use a white male actor for the part.

But modern theatre productions are moving away from stereotyping, giving white male parts to ethnic minority actors and women, and creating some memorable pieces of drama as a result.

Not what Shakespeare intended, perhaps, but then, what is? ■

POOR BOOK STOCK

The recent surge in sales of popular reading books for 7-12-year-olds has raised important questions about the availability of titles by black and ethnic authors in book shops.

A variety of books produced for adults have become more easily available, such as Zadie Smith's *White Teeth*. Yet children's choice often remains painfully limited to stories about gangs, rap music and slavery. One 15-year-old reader said in response to the current state of subjects available: 'I'm fed up reading books about Asian fathers forcing their young daughters to marry. Why can't people write about real life?'

The blame may not lie entirely with the writers or authors themselves, but rather with the people that run the book shops. Many companies now have sections in their stores called 'black interest', lumping together titles by 'black' authors. But how many can be read by younger readers? It seems that not enough is being done to promote or encourage the interests of black and ethnic readers. One store manager in West London said: 'We have tried to introduce more young, trendy fiction by black writers, and this does seem to have worked.'

This is not true, however, for all book shops. Many are more selective about which titles they stock. ■

Brit Storms New York

The young black Briton at the centre of a major row in America over freedom of expression stands to cash in. Chris Ofili, the 1998 Turner Prize winner, so outraged the Mayor of New York with his contribution to an exhibition staged at one of the city's leading museums, that the Mayor attempted to ban the show.

When the Brooklyn Museum decided to back Ofili and other Brit-artists in the *Sensation* show, engineered by the British collector Charles Saatchi, an interesting new precedent was set.

Mayor Guiliani put a stop to New York's grant to the Museum, and the Museum replied by suing him for breaching its First Amendment rights – the right to freedom of expression.

Ofili's expression was a Black Madonna portrait, adorned with elephant dung and cut-out body parts from pornographic magazines.

Now the Museum's robust defence of Ofili's work, and the media circus that blew up around the *Sensation* exhibition, ensured that his watercolours and dung-embellished canvasses flew off the walls at the New York gallery run by Gavin Brown.

The controversial Madonna, meanwhile, may need to be cleaned after a 72-year-old art critic expressed his disgust by smearing it with white paint. ■

Chris Ofili is a leading light among Britain's new generation of artists.

WALFORD IN THE ISLE-OF-DOGS HOUSE

Ever wondered what became of Sanjay and Gita, from *EastEnders*? In fact, ever wondered what became of the hundreds of thousands of London's east-enders from the subcontinent who never seem to turn up in Walford?

A new report for the Broadcasting Standards Council, *Include Me In*, gives a clue. Annabelle Sreberny-Mohammadi, of Leicester University's Centre for Mass Communications, has found that Asians remain terribly stereotyped and two-dimensional in television drama.

EAST-END LIES

In fact, characters have failed so miserably, the report found, that many Asian Britons would rather they weren't portrayed on screen than be shown-up by such useless, two-dimensional parts. Channel 4 and BBC2 were most likely to engage intelligently with the Asian viewer, the report finds, with BBC2's comedy sketch show *Goodness Gracious Me* achieving high approval among young Asians.

When will the missing Sanjay and Gita be replaced on BBC1's prime-time soap? Don't hold your breath! ■

London's east-end is a multicultural melting pot, unlike the soap opera EastEnders.

Closing the Net?

'Hate speech' on the Internet has long resisted control by governments. This has partly been due to a long-standing commitment to free speech in democratic countries. But it's also a technical issue.

Unwilling to look impotent in the face of technology, politicians who are usually keen to attack racist and other discriminatory language spent most of the 90s saying that they wouldn't intervene on the Net.

But the mood began to change recently, as both technical solutions and political agreement seemed to bring the policing of free speech on the Net within grasp. In September 1998, government minister Jack Straw spoke of his hope that the Net could be closed on 'abuse' by careful inter-national co-operation.

By April 1999, he felt able to tell the House of Commons that: 'Certainly, there is a problem with incitement [to racial hatred] on the Internet as its authors may come from outside our jurisdiction. We have actively considered this point, not least in the context of the fight against organised and international crime.'

INTERNET ABUSE

In October 2000, an Australian commission on human rights ruled some Holocaust 'denial' material removed from the Web. Kathleen McEvoy, head of the commission, ruled that: 'In public discourse there is a need to balance rights and responsibilities. It is never appropriate to victimise people of a certain race in the name of freedom of speech.'

While the politicians and lawyers are grappling with the constitutional issues, though, the Net is slowly closing on racists, as the companies which provide them with access to the physical network become more sensitive to being sued. Several sites have been closed down around the world in the last two years as a result of ISPs (Internet Service Providers) simply cancelling contracts they have with racist groups. ■

IS SHAFT BACK?

It's thirty years since the first *Shaft* hit the silver screen and revolu-tionised the role of black actors in the movies. Now *Shaft* is back, bigger, but not necessarily better. 'Blax-ploitation' – films designed to drag in the paying black audience – burst onto the big screens in 1971. The civil rights movement of the 1960s had opened the way for black Americans to participate in mainstream arts such as cinema.

Gordon Parks, a black photographer working for *Life* magazine, captured the moment with the first major Hollywood production directed by a black American. But *The Learning Tree* was a historical feature, and Parks wanted something that made black audiences cheer. With *Shaft*, he created a legend.

Parks described the film as 'a Saturday night fun picture which people go to because they want to see the black guy winning'. For years afterwards films featuring black actors traded on *Shaft*'s success. But once the novelty wore off, a more critical black audience began to reject such cheap cash-ins, and the genre faded away.

The new film has been rejected by most critics, with little to distinguish it from the old version. What certainly has changed, however, is the role of black artists. The original Shaft, legendary actor Richard Roundtree, was paid $13,000 for his starring role in the film. His successor, Samuel L. Jackson, reportedly netted a cool $10 million. ■

Notting Hill Conspiracy

The Editor

According to John Tyndall of the British National Front, the Notting Hill Carnival, the world-famous street party held annually in West London, is nothing more than a cultural propaganda exercise. Huge crowds of people from almost every ethnic background apparently get together as part of a carefully orchestrated media cover-up. Tyndall suggests it is organised to demonstrate the harmony of Britain's multicultural society, hiding the fact that Britain's cultural identity is at crisis point.

MEDIA COVER-UP?

According to Tyndall, British culture is being undermined by other influences, including Britain's mix of people from different ethnic backgrounds. He believes that races should be kept separate, and he promotes the idea that Britain should be for 'white' people only.

Fortunately, festivals such as the Notting Hill Carnival remind the rest of us that British culture is much more than a narrow-minded racially motivated idea. Sure, over time British culture has changed, but mainly for the better. However, violence such as the murders that occured at the Notting Hill Carnival 2000, while being the exception, can be used as propaganda. They add fuel to racist agendas such as that promoted by John Tyndall. ■

QUOTES

■ The constant vying between political parties about which is tougher on asylum numbers is sending out the message that refugees are a threat. Just as Enoch Powell's call for tighter immigration controls in the 1960s and 1970s led to an increase in racial violence, so today the same process is occurring. And this time, the situation is being made worse by the government's dispersal programme which leads to refugees being isolated and vulnerable.
Frances Webber, immigration barrister

■ Are you racist? No. We are simply asking for the same rights given to the other races without question in today's world – the right to keep one's homeland, identity and way of life.
BNP website, Frequently Asked Questions page

■ Celebrating minority cultures is a good thing but, in doing that, we've given them so much attention that we've become apologetic about the majority, mainstream culture ... the national curriculum has put a stop to many of the worst excesses, but some people have still lost sight of the idea that we belong to one country, and if membership is to mean anything, we have to have a common culture.
Nicholas Tate, Chief Executive of the Qualifications and Curriculum Authority

The Notting Hill Carnival has become a traditional part of West London life.

ETHNO-TOURISM COMES HOME

Should we be worrying about a growing trend for ethno-tourism, or does this suggest a world more open to sharing cultural differences?

'Post-colonial' tourism, in which holiday-makers from rich countries try to 'get to know' the cultures of people in less developed areas, is increasing.

The reasons are varied, but the tourist industry is aware that tourists are more likely to be interested in items of anothers' culture than they are in scenery or activities.

Tourism to Aboriginal lands in Australia, for example, has increased dramatically in recent years. But far from promoting cultural interaction, the highly-organised tours seem only to have distanced visitors from the people they came to meet.

On one well-known tour to Uluru – the Aboriginal name for Ayers Rock – the demonstration of traditional hunting skills and a kangaroo barbecue proved such a highlight that tour operators were very unhappy if a kangaroo failed to show up.

The Aborigines found a practical

solution by collecting one or two dead kangaroos from the roadside each morning. These could be popped-up from behind a bush to be felled by a boomerang. The tour operators were more than happy until one observant tourist spotted tyre-tracks on the kangaroo carcass.

Other people are less prepared to participate in this kind of tourism, and resent being treated like exhibits in a human zoo.

The Maori people of New Zealand have established firm rules for tourism in their homelands to protect their culture from souvenir hunters and nosy holiday-makers. An indigenous tribe in British Columbia, Canada, has even tried warning tourists off. A sign on one bridge linking their island to the mainland reads: 'If you have no business here, do not cross.'

But while Western tourists are bagging photos of rare and 'exotic' people, a strange process is gripping their own countries.

Eager for the tourist dollar/yen/baht, European countries are also playing up their cultural traditions. Britain's tourism industry largely depends on its recreation of Merrie Olde Englande/Scotlande/Wales, in which kilted souvenir Highland dolls can be bought at an authentic stall in London, just in case you miss the coach for the day trip to Edinburgh.

Which country, in the end, is most embarrassed by ethno-tourism? ∎

ROCK ON

Uluru, the landscape feature once known outside Australia as Ayers Rock, is back under the management of Australia's first people, the Aborigines.

After a claim was lodged in 1979 by the Pitjantjatjara and Yankuntjatjara people, the wheels were set in motion for the rock to be officially handed back to the Aborigines in 1985. Since that time there have been some changes to the tourism experience, mostly for the better.

Uluru is an Aboriginal sacred site. Because of this tourists are now encouraged not to scale the 1.6km to the top. Also, over the years a pathway became worn into the rock as tourists walked up it, leading to fears of further erosion if it wasn't stopped.

Vistors can, however, enjoy a tour of sacred sites around Uluru's base, hearing fascinating tales from Aboriginal oral mythology. You can still have a moving experience just by looking at Uluru and you'll be contributing to the preservation of a natural global monument as well. ∎

Australia's famous natural landmark has, not for the first time, changed hands.

Olympics Honour Aborigines

The Sports Editor

The Olympic Gold medallist Cathy Freeman has won herself a place in her nation's heart.

The runner, who also lit the ceremonial torch at the start of the Sydney Olympic Games, has come to mean something powerful to her fellow Aborigines, once a hidden minority in Australia.

In taking such a leading role in the Olympics, Freeman showed that Australia is no longer trying to hide its difficult history of race relations. Her many fans see her as a symbol of hope for the Aboriginal people.

Freeman was born in 1973, and won her first gold medal at the Commonwealth Games in 1994.

FREE SPIRIT

It was here that her role as an icon for the Aboriginal cause took off – she took her lap of honour with both an Australian and an Aboriginal flag. This symbol of Aboriginal pride offended the Australian team's boss, Arthur Tunstall, and a national debate followed their public disagreement.

Ever since, Cathy has carried the torch for hundreds of thousands of Aborigines, who were at one time hunted for sport by white settlers. She has called attention to the 'stolen generation' – around 100,000 Aboriginal children forcibly removed from their parents and adopted by white families and church institutions in the first half of the 20th century. Her own family was torn apart by this policy.

Cathy Freeman's rise to fame represents a possible change in fortunes for all Aborigines. State parliaments have apologised for their part in programmes which attacked Aboriginal culture, and white Australia is more accepting of the Aboriginal cause than ever before.

Even Arthur Tunstall has conceded a little way: in a recent advertisement for tea, Cathy Freeman asks him 'Would you like your tea white, Arthur?', to which the old man replies 'Black will be fine.' ∎

Flag Cannot Be Tucked Away

The designer of the Aboriginal flag, Harold Thomas, has news for those who hope the symbol will replace the Union Jack in the corner of Australia's national flag. Mr Thomas, who designed the Aboriginal flag in 1971 has said that what it represents shouldn't be treated as a 'secondary thing', tucked away in a corner. ∎

Cathy Freeman's victory lap with the Aboriginal flag made her a campaigning icon.

AUDLEY IS NEW HOPE

British boxer Audley Harrison continued a long tradition of black British athletic success at the Sydney Olympics with his gold medal. Harrison, who led a slightly wayward life as a teenager, made good through the discipline and creativity of his chosen sport.

Having admired the boxing film *Rocky*, aged 13, Harrison got into some minor trouble in West London and ended up with a brief custodial sentence. It gave him time to reflect on where he wanted to go, and boxing provided the answer.

Though he still trains to the soundtrack from *Rocky*, Harrison is definitely a man motivated by his own priorities. With his eye on the heavyweight championship of the world, Harrison also looks forward to life beyond the ring. Many Britons secretly hope he'll be taking that belt with him. ■

Harrison grabs gold with a knockout performance.

GOALKEEPER FINED FOR NAZI SALUTE

The referee doesn't see the funny side of Bosnich's 'joke'.

The controversial goalkeeper Mark Bosnich continued his travels around England's Premiership clubs in 2001 with a move to Chelsea.

The Aussie international made his name with Manchester United and Aston Villa in the early 90s, with an estimable clean sheet record. But Bosnich has always been dogged by controversy, particularly since the British press branded him a Nazi.

The keeper had been involved in a long-running spat with Tottenham Hotspur fans about a clash between himself and their top striker Jurgen Klinsmann. But he repaid the Spurs jibes (serenading him with 'Klinsmann Wonderland') with a Nazi salute.

This earned him a yellow card, a £1,000 fine from the Football Association, a demand from MP Glyn Ford that he be kicked out of football and a brief police investigation before the Crown Prosecution Service decided to drop charges. Many commentators noted that Spurs is historically associated with Jewish supporters in London, and one newspaper even hinted that Bosnich's Croatian roots might explain his alleged fascism.

Bosnich himself was bemused. He explained in an open letter that he had simply been mimicking the TV sitcom character Basil Fawlty, and had only humorous intentions. ■

WHO'S WHO

Here are just some of the groups committed to the promotion of race awareness, education and news. They provide a good starting point for further study, including links and addresses to many other organisations.

UNITED KINGDOM

■ Anti-Nazi League
Broad based organisation aiming to stop Nazi's reaching a wider audience and growing. PO Box 2566, London N4 1WJ
Telephone: 020 7924 0333
http://www.anl.org.uk

■ Black Britain Online
Part of the Colourful Network, providing information for the UK black African-Caribbean community. Thames House, South Bank Commercial Centre, 140 Battersea Park Road, London SW11 4NB
Telephone: 020 7498 5656
http://www.blackbritain.co.uk

■ Black Information Link
Platform for Asian, African and Caribbean information exchange. Southbank Technopark, 90 London Road, London SE1 6LN
http://www.blink.org.uk

■ Britkid
A web game about race, racism and life – also contains a section on education.
http://www.britkid.org

■ Commission for Racial Equality
Publicly funded body that works in partnership with individuals and organisations for a fair and just society. Elliot House, 10-12 Allington Street, London SW1E 5EH
Telephone: 020 7828 7022
http://www.cre.gov.uk

■ Joint Council for the Welfare of Immigrants
An independent national voluntary organisation campaigning for justice and combating racism. 115 Old Street, London EC1V 9RT
http://www.jcwi.org.uk

■ Searchlight
Web version of the magazine aimed at combating racism and facism. 37B New Cavendish Street, London W1M 8JR
http://www.searchlightmagazine.com

■ Show Racism the Red Card
An organisation providing news, free information and links on tackling racism in sport. PO Box 141, Whitley Bay NE26 3YH
http://www.srtrc.org

INTERNATIONAL

■ Artists Against Racism
Campaign group that aims to build an understanding of all people. AAR International, Box 54511, Toronto, Ontario, Canada M5M 4N5
http://www.artistsagainstracism.com

■ Ethnic Communities Council of NSW Inc
Aims to increase understanding of the social and economic benefits of cultural diversity amongst the general community. 221 Cope Street, Waterloo NSW 2017
http://www.eccnsw.org.au

■ European Research Centre on Migration and Ethnic Relations
Group promoting academic research in ethnic relations, racism and ethnic conflict within Europe. ERCOMER, Utrecht University, Heidelberglaan 2, 3584 CS Utrecht, The Netherlands
http://www.ercomer.org

■ Human Rights and Equal Opportunites Commission
Publicly funded, independent Australian body which monitors and investigates issues including racial discrimimantion and Aboriginal social justice. Level 8, Piccadilly Tower, 133 Castlereagh Street, Sydney, NSW 2000
http://www.humanrights.gov.au

■ Race Relations Office
177 Queen Street, Auckland, New Zealand. Telephone: 09 307 2352

■ Racism: No way!
Australian project which aims to assist school communities in recognising and addressing racism in the learning environment. PO Box 590, Darlinghurst NSW 2010
http://www.racismnoway.com.au

GO ON, TALK ABOUT IT

The Racism News doesn't just want to give you its views on the news. It wants you, its readers, to talk about the issues too. Here are some questions to get you started:

■ How do you think the Stephen Lawrence Inquiry has affected you?
■ Should people be given jobs or school places because of government policy or individual ability?

■ What can be done to improve the role of the police in race relations?
■ Why do people join racist groups like the British National Party?
■ What could be done to improve the way Britain deals with asylum seekers?
■ Should freedom of speech be preserved on the Internet, even if it means racist ideas can be promoted?
■ Why should we let asylum seekers stay in the country?

■ What makes a multicultural society a better place to live, as opposed to one based on nationalist ideas?
■ Are immigrants to blame for shortages in housing, healthcare and other services?
■ What examples can you find of racist ideas in the media. How can you tell they are racist?
■ Can society ever become entirely free of racism. What can you do to help?